IRELAND'S HOUSING CRISIS

IRELAND'S HOUSING CRISIS

A Marxist analysis

John McAnulty

Ireland's housing crisis Copyright © 2018 by John McAnulty

Cover designed by O Nic Lochlainn

First Printing: Aug 2018
Socialist Democracy, Belfast Ireland

www.socialistdemocracy.org

Copies of this book have been lodged with the British Library and the National Library of Ireland

ISBN: 9781981070824

Many Thanks to:

O Nic Lochlainn
(Cover design and the essay *Capitalist Recovery: Making people Homeless*)
J M Thorne
The nature of Ireland's housing crisis
J Fearon
Ireland's new Landlordism
O Nic Lochlainn and J Davids
The housing crisis in the North of Ireland

CONTENTS

Introduction 9
Setting the scene 11
The cost of housing 15
Capitalist Recovery: Making people Homeless. 19
The nature of Ireland's housing crisis 23
-Ireland's new Landlordism 31
The housing crisis in the North of Ireland 39
A radical movement, a radical strategy: 43

INTRODUCTION

Ireland has been held up as the poster child of the European austerity era. Alone it stepped forward to offer a full guarantee to bankers and bondholders, bankrupting itself in the process.

Despite widespread public anger it offered no serious resistance to the austerity agenda, no resistance to Troika control of the economy, and accepted a modernisation programme of sell-off of local resources and mass privatisation.

The country is now proclaimed as proof of the efficiency of the austerity medicine. For a number of years it has led economic growth in Europe. Business continues to boom and transnational funds to flow in.

Yet there is much to question. Irish workers lost 10% of their wages and pensions and these have only partly been restored. In the public sector a two tier wage system operates, with those entering employment during the austerity period being paid at much less than the standard rate. The fiscal space available for public spending is constrained by European regulation and by the ongoing need to pay sovereign debt - an issue until 2054. As a result the proclaimed end of austerity has left the majority of public services in tatters. Education is underfunded and health in permanent crisis.

Above all housing is in a state of collapse. In addition to the lack of public investment a sizeable amount of financial activity impacts negatively on housing.

Property taken into public ownership by Nama is now sold off in a series of fire sales to vulture capitalists who then help to push up housing costs to recover their investment. At the same time landlordism remains a sizeable element of native economic activity and the lack of regulation plus government subsidy leads to price inflation. The government proposed to increase housebuilding by legalising new investment through Real Estate Investment Trusts. The result has been a surge in profits for the new vehicles and little in the way of new build. There are no serious plans for public housing – all attention is fixed on developers who promise to offer affordable housing.

All of the above is a partial description of life in Ireland from a Marxist perspective. However, as Marx himself said, the point is to change things and to do this we have to look at the existing opposition.

The focus of protest is the Irish Congress of Trade Unions. ICTU protested the swingeing austerity but did not oppose it. They suggested amendments to budgets to correct what they saw as excessive damage to the very poor, but overall helped implement wage and service cuts and implemented austerity. The trade unions mobilised supporters only to head off criticism or to lobby for specific programs carefully constructed to prove affordability within the austerity budget. The slogan was "a better fairer way." The banks and bondholders would have to be paid, but there was an unspecified third way to do so without any pain.

Socialist groups have followed a nonaggression pact with the union bureaucracy, focusing instead on recruitment to their own organisations and battles for parliamentary representation.

In the decades since the collapse of armed activity and acceptance of the peace process Sinn Fein have become a constitutional nationalist party indistinguishable from the other parties.

The current opposition shares with the government a common myth: that Ireland is an independent capitalist country. By focusing on the political economy of housing we hope to show that, on the contrary, Ireland is a country dominated by imperialism and the local capitalists act as clients for it, deforming the Irish economy and impoverishing Irish workers.

The construction of a serious opposition, in my view, hangs on gaining wider acceptance of an anti-imperialist analysis.

SETTING THE SCENE

This examination of the Irish housing crisis, as with any other analysis, has a context. The context here is based on a class analysis using the methodology developed by Karl Marx and Frederick Engels.

In extremely compressed form the Marxian thesis is as follows:

Capitalism is a system of exploitation centred on the junction of capital and labour to produce value. The process of exploitation is largely invisible. The worker is apparently free to accept or reject employment and to negotiate a fair wage, but their labour power produces extra value above and beyond the process of production that belongs to the capitalist.

The output of the labour process is the commodity. In it is the self-evident use value that leads us to purchase it and also a separate exchange value in the market which allows for profit. Exploitation is not restricted to production. As part of the circuit of capital value has to be realized in the market place. A constant struggle to extract more value means that exploitation of the worker occurs as commodities are bought and sold also.

At the point of its birth Marx warned that the capitalist system was inherently unstable and would eventually decay. An inbuilt business cycle sees boom followed by bust. Across the cycles the battles between capitalists lead to a struggle for profit and a greater and greater investment in "dead" labour contained in machinery and less in actual workers. As value is created by workers, over time the overall rate of profit tends to fall.

Capitalism has constantly adapted to survive. Manufacturing capital became banking capital and they fused to become finance capital. Small firms became giant monopolies. World wars were fought to obtain wealth from colonies conquered by force and former colonies were then integrated into a world imperialist system. In the process peasants and sections of the middle classes have been forced into the working class and an immense transfer of wealth has taken place, with a tiny number controlling global wealth while the vast majority are impoverished. The world is fractured into a few imperialist powers, smaller powers that huddle together for protection, and semi-colonies that submit to imperialist order.

At one stage it was believed that the immense productivity unleashed by capital would liberate humanity. Instead we see a growing gulf between rich and poor. Many still put their hope in the state to reverse this process. A progressive government could use the state to bring about fairness and equality.

As with so much else in capitalism, the claim that a neutral state stands above contending classes is an illusion. The state, as with everything else in capitalist society, is an instrument of class rule. This rule is enforced directly through an army and police force but also the state has to act to impose order on a chaotic market system or to make concessions in the face of worker's mobilisations.

In their day-to-day running parliaments are usually centres of bribery and corruption. Many are controlled by a few wealthy clans or by the agents of the great powers. Much of the control of society is in the hands of unelected officials. When a truly progressive government is formed it is either overthrown by force or frustrated through legal and financial pressures.

The belief that the state can correct for the inequalities of capitalism comes mainly from an era of capitalist boom and working class resurgence following the Second World War. That belief cannot hold in the present era of capitalist decay.

The current global disintegration and instability are best understood as heralding the death agony of capitalism. The mass of wealth in the world is growing greater while approximately 50% of the working class across the world are unemployed, the potential for a high rate of profit continues to fall and the financialisation of capital sees endless attempts to breed money from money without any link to production and a constant raiding of public resource and funds to recover from the inevitable failures. Unthinking exploitation of the environment, a "free" source of industrial inputs and outputs, is now unsustainable. The future holds either a transition to a socialist society or a descent into barbarism.

Ireland is a unique case. Part of Europe, the north-east section remains occupied by Britain. The southern component is a semi-colony, with economic activity dominated by implantation of transnational capital. This influx was on such a scale that it was followed by the speculative "Celtic Tiger" boom followed by economic collapse where the government literally bankrupted the country to guarantee loans by banks and bondholders. A long period of austerity followed, which involved direct rule by a Troika of the European Commission, Central Bank and IMF. Today a massive sovereign debt and overarching European regulation still constrain the social expenditure. In the North a rickety economy is feeling the impact of its own major austerity initiative – the Fresh start initiative. The chaos is made greater by the collapse of the political settlement manufactured by Blair and Clinton and by unionist support for Brexit – a process that will restore a hard border and further beggar the local economy.

The southern economy runs on two parallel tracks. The minor element is the native economy, still largely dependent on the British economy and vulnerable to Brexit. The major track of the economy is transnational capital, much of it attracted by Ireland's status as a tax haven, and increasingly dominated by speculative financial capital.

It is only necessary to add that Ireland, with less than 1% of Europe's population, agreed to pay 46% of the European banking debt - a debt that will remain until 2054.

It has been claimed that austerity and submission to Europe were successful strategies and that Ireland is now the fastest growing economy in Europe. Yet pay rates have fallen 10% during the austerity, the Troika programme remains and constrains public expenditure in a narrow "fiscal space" while enforcing a modernisation programme of deregulation and privatisation. This shaky edifice is now facing a second tsunami of personal debt, focused on housing and rolling forward on ruling class landlordism, European debt regulation and speculative Vulture capitalism.

THE COST OF HOU' sugre

A ny assessment of the housing crisis, both in Ireland and across the world, should start with two simple observations.

The first is that the majority cost of housing is in the inflation of land prices. In Ireland it accounts for the majority of the costs of new housing. The second observation is that land, by itself, has no value. As with air and water, it is a natural resource. Landlordism is not capitalism. At some stage force has been used to seize and enclose land and force is an ongoing factor in holding the land and expelling unwanted tenants. One of the major factors in the original conquest of Ireland and in many other colonies was the inability of the native population to deal with the concept of land as personal property.

In the era of capitalism land and the property on it act as a store of "fictional capital" that can no longer be invested productively. Nowhere does the old anarchist adage "property is theft" carry more weight.

Many will shrug their shoulders at this as an historical footnote from the writings of the Irish revolutionary James Connolly, yet today apartments are being built in the major cities of the world, not for habitation, but as stores of wealth for the 1%. Working class districts are seeing mass eviction of residents in a process of gentrification. In Ireland an historical experiment is taking place. Massive property portfolios, bankrolled by the workers and held in the state National Asset Management Agency (NAMA) fund are, as part of a firesale, transferred to "Vulture Capital" funds based in New York. This transfer is government policy, surrounded by corruption and payoffs to officials and politicians. A notable example is the bulk sale of assets in the northern colony, where resources with a book value of 11 billion euro were sold for 4 billion. A member of the NAMA board also represented the vulture capital funds purchasing the assets and several million appeared in an offshore account, allegedly destined for the pockets of a local unionist leader. The scheme was designed to speed up payments to the European Central Bank. The Vulture funds are not required to pay tax and the only discussion hangs around whether or not they should be bound by what little housing and rental regulation there is – the

THE COST OF HOUSING

Any assessment of the housing crisis, both in Ireland and across the world, should start with two simple observations.

The first is that the majority cost of housing is in the inflation of land prices. In Ireland it accounts for the majority of the costs of new housing. The second observation is that land, by itself, has no value. As with air and water, it is a natural resource. Landlordism is not capitalism. At some stage force has been used to seize and enclose land and force is an ongoing factor in holding the land and expelling unwanted tenants. One of the major factors in the original conquest of Ireland and in many other colonies was the inability of the native population to deal with the concept of land as personal property.

In the era of capitalism land and the property on it act as a store of "fictional capital" that can no longer be invested productively. Nowhere does the old anarchist adage "property is theft" carry more weight.

Many will shrug their shoulders at this as an historical footnote from the writings of the Irish revolutionary James Connolly, yet today apartments are being built in the major cities of the world, not for habitation, but as stores of wealth for the 1%. Working class districts are seeing mass eviction of residents in a process of gentrification. In Ireland an historical experiment is taking place. Massive property portfolios, bankrolled by the workers and held in the state National Asset Management Agency (NAMA) fund are, as part of a firesale, transferred to "Vulture Capital" funds based in New York. This transfer is government policy, surrounded by corruption and payoffs to officials and politicians. A notable example is the bulk sale of assets in the northern colony, where resources with a book value of 11 billion euro were sold for 4 billion. A member of the NAMA board also represented the vulture capital funds purchasing the assets and several million appeared in an offshore account, allegedly destined for the pockets of a local unionist leader. The scheme was designed to speed up payments to the European Central Bank. The Vulture funds are not required to pay tax and the only discussion hangs around whether or not they should be bound by what little housing and rental regulation there is – the planning laws means more congestion. Cutting regulation and reducing the space required for homes means paying through the nose for instant slums.

This is Famine thinking. During the famine food was exported from Ireland. Landlords could not picture a world where their rights did not take precedence. Today our property is handed to the vultures while we suffer.

Conor Skehan is right to say that the housing market will regulate itself. What he neglects to mention is that it will regulate itself to maximize profit. It will do nothing for those homeless and those evicted and expelled.

One of the main jobs of the capitalist state is to mitigate the effects of the market and head off the revolts that it would provoke, but above all the state defends the bankers, the landlords and the vulture capitalists. In Ireland there has never been the accumulation of native capital that would allow a fullblown programme of social housing. Much initial capital was "gombeen" (accumulated interest from rents and agricultural loans). Landlordism was an initial direction for native capital and it evolved into a highly corrupt system where politicians arranged rezoning of land in exchange for bribes, land was sold at knockdown prices and in return speculators would build a small proportion of social or affordable homes to justify the land giveaway. In the Celtic Tiger years the exploitation involved in this system was multiplied by subsidies to bankers, developers and speculators while workers paid through taxes and then again through inflated mortgages. In the aftermath the government, despite its claims, acts under the direction of the Troika and the constraints of European regulation. There is no room in the fiscal space for mass public spending. That means that the government's main concern will be to throw dust in our faces and convince us they are taking action while doing little.

The underlying reality of a parasitic capitalist class, of Ireland's status as a semi-colony and of Europe's role as a ferocious defender of profit in a period of instability and weak recovery means that many traditional reforms will not be effective. Calling for government action in general will simply lead to further attempts to stimulate profit and a greater crisis. Calls for a mass programme of social housing recognise worker's needs but come up against the reality that the current system cannot and will not adopt the necessary measures.

Ireland has lived under a decade of austerity and shouldered a crippling debt. Workers have lived through this decade and accepted quite severe restriction on their standard of living in the belief that the recovery will generate economic advances that will eventually be shared out. The political expression of this was the Landsdowne Road ll public sector deal that limited pay and pension restoration and retained a two-tier public sector pay structure, with new entrants paid much less.

At its heart the eye-watering charges for rents and mortgages, the savage punishment of those in arrears, are mechanisms that operate as a sort of negative wage, taking a greater and greater proportion of earnings that go, along with so much else, in a continuing the unending payment to the banks. Yet the government and ICTU union leadership negotiated a new Lansdowne Road agreement that keeps austerity in place but releases just enough public sector pay to head off explosion. The upward march of housing costs threatens to undo the social peace and turn a humanitarian crisis into a full-blown political crisis where workers reject the meagre slice of the pie allocated to them.

So a housing campaign should be firmly anti-imperialist, recognising that we are in a fight to the death with the government, the vulture funds and the Troika. Housing for all would involve the rejection of the ongoing sovereign debt and expropriation of vulture capitalist property alongside the seizure of NAMA properties and their conversion to housing. In these circumstances we should return to the 2016 Apollo house strategy, when a NAMA property was seized by trade unionists and community activists and converted for use by the homeless. We should work from above and below demanding action from the government while at the same time being willing to take control of our own property and use it for our own needs.

Begging imperialism to show mercy is no alternative to a real fight.

CAPITALIST RECOVERY: MAKING PEOPLE HOMELESS.

In late 2007 and early 2008 we became aware of an economic time bomb exploding on Wall Street then sending a shock wave through the global economy. The first phase of the economic shock was traced to the subprime loan market for property, both commercial and residential. The dominant banks had gambled on ever rising property prices guaranteeing ever returning income, the returns dependent on gigantic loans made to the great property magnates. The expanded economic shock wave called forth emergency action by all of the central banks. Governments, taking their advice exclusively from the leading central bankers, moved quickly to contain the crisis by taking over the defaulting investments of the banks and property magnates. The central banks and the governments did indeed slow the economic shake wave but at a great social cost to the rest of society and especially to the living conditions of the working class.

The government of Ireland acted to stave off a banking collapse with a taxpayer's bailout, socialising the speculative losses incurred by the dominant banks. The Irish Sovereign Debt to GDP ratios rose from 25% of National Income in 2007 to 125% in 2013. Never in the history of any modern state finance had there been such a generous hand out to such a tiny section of the population. To facilitate the bailing out of the banks and property magnates the Irish Government set in motion a whole raft of measures to expropriate 'spare' income form public sector workers and individual households. The official position of the Irish Government was and still is that everything that was done to save the fortunes of the tiny minority was absolutely necessary and their constant refrain today is that the bailout succeeded, for the Irish 'Real' economy is back in rude health. However there is the not so forgettable matter of the grim after life of the property boom and bust.

Much has been said about fake news. The worst of fake news of course emanates from Governments, with a constant outpouring of fake news pertaining to the state of the economy. The core of economic fake news is that a recovery for capital and the capitalist class also means a return to prosperity for the working class. The capitalist economy in GDP terms has recovered in America and in Europe, meaning capitalism is no longer in recession, but for the working class there is precious little evidence of a recovery. One reason for this is that capitalism underwent a change in the period of neo liberal hegemony; capital moved away from investing in manufacturing and productive services and moved into investing in property in a very big way. Here we will draw on evidence put together in a recently published book *'Rethinking the Economics of Land and Housing'* by Collins, Lloyd and McFarland.

Although their evidence is drawn primarily from the British context there can be little doubt that the findings would work for all those economies that follow the neo-liberal recipe book for economic recovery. Quoting directly from the British Office for National Statistics, they show that since 1995 net economic value has risen by some £7 trillion, yet when the figures are analysed we discover that over £5 trillion of the increase is attributed to the market value of what the ONS calls dwellings. The value of dwellings is then broken down into two parts, the value of the buildings and the value of the land the buildings rest on. What we then discover is that the value of the Land grabs some £4 trillion of the increase, meaning in the last two decades the value of land has increased fourfold.

For those who own property, this has provided enormous benefits. According to the Resolution Foundation, homeowners born in the 1940s and 1950s gained an unearned windfall of £80,000 between 1993 and 2014 alone. In the early 2000s, house price growth was so great that 17% of working-age adults earned more from their house than from their job.

As house prices have continued to increase and the gap between house prices and earnings has grown larger, the cost of home ownership has become increasingly prohibitive. Whereas in the mid-1990s low and middle income households could afford a first time buyer deposit after saving for around 3 years, today it takes the same households 20 years to save for a deposit. Many have increasingly found themselves with little choice but to rent privately. For those stuck in the private rental market, the proportion of income spent on housing costs has risen from around 10% in 1980 to 36% today. Unlike homeowners, there is no asset wealth to draw on to fund new cars or holidays.

We have yet to confront the truth about the trillions of pounds of wealth amassed through the housing market in recent decades: this wealth has come straight out of the pockets of those who don't own property.

When the value of a house goes up, the total productive capacity of the economy is unchanged because nothing new has been produced: it merely constitutes an increase in the value of the land underneath. We have known since the days of Adam Smith and David Ricardo that land is not a source of wealth but of economic rent — a means of extracting wealth from others. Or as Joseph Stiglitz puts it;

> *"getting a larger share of the pie rather than increasing the size of the pie".*

The truth is that much of the wealth accumulated in recent decades has been gained at the expense of those who will see more of their incomes eaten up by higher rents and larger mortgage payments.

Misleading accounting and irresponsible economics have provided cover for this heist. The government's national accounts record house price growth as new wealth, ignoring the cost it imposes on others in society – particularly young people and those yet to be born. Economists still hail house price inflation as a sign of economic strength.

This is what we can legitimately name fake prosperity. What the evidence refutes is the often-articulated argument that what society has to do is to build many more dwellings, for nearly all of the financial speculation and inflation comes primarily from the rising land values, and not from the rising value of dwellings. The problem socialists have to confront is less the lack of new builds; in Britain and Ireland there are tens of thousands of empty dwellings. It is more like the monopoly ownership of land forcing up the value of both new and old builds. One of the great differences between the classical political economists and those that came later, whom Karl Marx called the vulgar economists, is that the classical economists understood the importance of the ownership of land for the health of the economy:

The early pioneers of political economy – Adam Smith, David Ricardo and John Stuart Mill –acknowledged that land had unique qualities, distinct from capital and labour. They recognised that land was a free gift of nature, and considered returns earned from the ownership of land to be unearned – referring to these windfalls as 'economic rent'. They believed that the ability to extract economic rent was so powerful that landowners could effectively absorb much of the value created in an economy. It was feared that this could undermine the political legitimacy of the private property system itself, and so they sought to limit the extent to which landowners could make unearned windfall gains at the expense of the rest of society.

The classical economists would have called what has been happening Fake Prosperity, they would have referred to it as unearned income and rent transfer from one social class to another, yet today the authoritative economists, the economic pundits and, most important of all, the Governments, celebrate what the classical economists frowned upon and sought to outlaw through progressive legislation and taxation.

One of the pioneering demands of the first socialist movement was for a common ownership of the Land, this demand has been forgotten, but it is as important now as it ever was.

THE NATURE OF IRELAND'S HOUSING CRISIS

The housing crisis housing is not a natural disaster or a result of mistaken policy but rather the result of changes in the economy – reinforced by specific housing and economic policies pursued by successive governments – that have favoured one class over another. It is this theme of class inequality that runs through every aspect of the housing crisis.

The figures on inequality and housing are stark. There were 1,400 homeless families and 2,500 children in emergency accommodation across the state. At the same time 198,358 homes (about 13% of total housing stock) lie empty. In Cork, there are 269 people homeless, and 21,287 vacant units and in Dublin, 3,247 people homeless and 35,293 vacant homes. Waiting lists for social housing and private rental accommodation grow as the price of housing is inflated higher and higher. At the most exclusive end of the residential market so called "trophy homes" exchange hands for over €4 million. Over 77,000 households are still in mortgage arrears while the debt of the developers that owed billions has been written off by NAMA and the banks. All these figures on housing come from the year 2016, a year which saw the number of millionaires in Ireland rise by five thousand. The critical point here is not just that there is inequality in housing but that the prosperity enjoyed by one class is dependent on the relative poverty of another. While this is true in all capitalist societies it is especially true in Ireland where housing and property have been a key source of wealth for the capitalist class. This is reflected in concentration of ownership with the richest 10% of the population owning 82% of all land (by value). Just 10% of households own 28% of the private housing stock. Within this top bracket ownership is concentrated even further - a mere 6,400 people own 156,500 properties. This means that just 0.004% of the population own 8% of the houses.   In recent years the anti-capitalist slogan of the 1% may have become a bit of a cliché but in Ireland - at least in relation to land and housing - it is not so far form the truth.

While the term "housing crisis" is useful as a general description we also need to examine the distinct elements of the crisis to get a better understanding of it.

It is in the private rental sector that the crisis is at its most acute. The main diver for this is **rising rents**. This trend - which is making renting increasingly unaffordable and insecure - is also feeding into other elements of the housing crisis such as homelessness and overcrowding.   Between 2011 and 2016 the average weekly rent paid to private landlords rose from €171.19 to €199.92, an increase of 16.8 per cent. The number of households paying at least €300 per week rent to a private landlord has increased 166% since 2011. It is also the case that rent rises in urban centres have been significantly higher than the national average.   For example, over the same period Dublin City saw a rise of almost 30% with the level of rents now 23% higher than they were at the peak of the "Celtic Tiger" property boom in 2008. Daft.ie, an Irish property website, reported recently that the average monthly rent in central Dublin is now €1,819 ($2,155)—more than 60% of the average pre-tax private-sector income. And it's not just Dublin - rent rises of over 20% have also been recorded in Dún Laoghaire– Rathdown (26.2%), Fingal (22.8%), South Dublin (22.7%) and Kildare (20.3%).

One of the consequences of rising rents is that an increasing proportion of people's incomes is going towards housing costs. For example, a single person on the average wage paying the average rent for a one bedroom apartment in Dublin is allocating 41% of their net income to the cost of renting. For a person on €25,000 (just above the media wage of €23,000) the proportion of net income going towards rent rises to fifty five percent. A further consequence of rising rents is the growing gap between the limits on housing benefit available for people on low incomes and the actual level of rents - a trend has put more that 80% of the homes available for rent beyond the financial reach of people in this category.

The other main feature of the private rental sector in Ireland is a lack of security for tenants. Regulation is minimal and enforcement of the few regulations that do exist is very weak. Landlords can evict tenants on the back of a claim that they are selling a property, moving in a family member or simply on the basis that a tenant is unable to pay an increased rent. These rules have increasingly been used by landlords as a means to evict tenants and get in new ones on higher rents.

Rapidly rising rents in the private sector are the most important driver within the housing crisis - not just because of the high number of people directly affected but also due the impact this is having all the other elements of that crisis. It is not a coincidence that over the period of rising rents from 2011 onwards there also has been an 81% increase in the number of people who are homeless; or that that number of people living in overcrowded homes has risen to 10% of the population. These statistics to not sit independently alongside one another - rather there is a direct causal link between them.

The second element of the housing crisis relates to house prices and **affordability**. While house prices are not at the level they were at the height of the property boom they have been rising steadily over recent years. From a trough in 2013 house prices across the state have increased by almost fifty percent. In urban centres that rise has been even greater with prices in Dublin increasing by 65% over the same period. This has major implications for the affordability of homes. While the term "affordable housing" is often used very loosely it is technically defined as three and half times a person's gross income. For two people on the average wage, this is about €245,000, and for two people on the median wage, €189,000. Currently the average price nationally is €250,000, while in Dublin it is €400,000. Both figures are well beyond the affordability ratio with the latter figure equating to seven times the gross income for a couple both on the medium wage.

A consequence of rising house prices (as with rising rents) is an increasing proportion of people's incomes going to housing costs. The point at which this is considered onerous - known as the Housing Cost Overburden Rate - is a household where the total housing costs represent more than 40% of the total disposable household income. Even households that are below this rate (where spending housing is more than 30% of disposable income) are considered at risk of facing an affordability problem. It is also the case that the extent to which housing is unaffordable is closely aligned to economic inequality with significant differences in the housing affordability rates for lower income households and higher income households. For example, the proportion of households below 60% of the median income affected by a housing cost overburden is nine times that of households above 60% of the median income. Over the period of the crisis the proportion of households in the low income category affected by cost overburden has incarcerated from 12% to 18% (some 150,000 households). While affordability is often presented as a generational issue that effects young people more than the old, economic inequality still cuts across age differences with young people on lower incomes more severely affected by the issue of housing affordability than young people on higher incomes.

The third main element of the housing crisis is **homelessness**. This is often the aspect of the crisis that gets the most attention given the dire circumstances that people in this category find themselves - whether that is living in emergency accommodation or sleeping on the streets. Homelessness has increased dramatically in Ireland over recent years. The number of people homeless in Ireland more than doubled from 3,226 to 7,421 between July 2014 and December 2016. A significant portion of this increase is accounted for by growing family homelessness. Of the families that are homeless a majority are lone parents who comprise 70% of the families in emergency accommodation. In the last year alone the number of homeless families increased by forty per cent and this category now numbers nearly 10,000 people including 3,755 children.

The number of homeless families in Dublin has increased by 289% over the period of the crisis with almost 700 families living in temporary and emergency accommodation. Much is totally unsuitable with families being unable to access cooking facilities and having to travel extended distances in order to bring their children to their school. Despite it designation as "emergency" and "temporary" this type of accommodation is becoming a long term response to the problem of homelessness.

The critical point to be made about homelessness is that it does not exist independently from rising rents and affordability. Indeed, it is evictions from the private rental sector and repossessions linked to mortgage arrears that are the main drivers of homelessness. In the interaction between the different elements of the housing crisis homelessness is more of a consequence than a cause. Of course the implication of this is that the crisis cannot be addressed by focusing solely on the issue of homelessness.

Despite the overwhelming evidence - in the form of objective statistics and the subjective testimony of individuals and families - of the existence of a housing crisis in Ireland there are still those at an official level who deny this reality. We had the claim by the chair of the Housing Agency (the government body set up in 2010 to advise on policy for housing) Conor Skehan that the problems Ireland was experiencing with housing were "completely normal" and just a phase of a market cycle that would soon correct itself. This followed on from an earlier claim by the same official that many people in emergency accommodation were not in genuine need but actually gaming the system. Such a dismissive attitude has also been echoed at a government level with the assertion by Taoiseach Leo Varadkar that homelessness in Ireland is low by international standards.

While the denial and downplaying of the housing crisis flies in the face of reality it does reveal the character of a political elite who are completely subservient to the demands of a class that has benefitted enormously from the hardships borne by others. To acknowledge the severity of the crisis would be to concede not only their inability to tackle it but also their complicity in pursuing policies that brought it about and are currently making it worse.

Within mainstream commentary the property boom, the financial crash and now the housing crisis are often put down to an Irish obsession with owning property. However, this superficial explanation bears little resemblance to reality. Up until the early 1960's home ownership in Ireland was quite low. In fact in 1961 only 25% of the population of urban areas lived in private housing; by 1986 this figure stood at 75%. This reason for this shift is not to be found in the Irish psyche but in the changes that were taking place in the capitalist economy in the 1970's and 80's which, in response to a decline in profitability - saw a shift of capital from production to finance. A key element of this was the transformation of homes into financial assets through privatisation and deregulation. This was epitomised by Margaret Thatcher's counter revolution in Britain which saw an all-out assault on public ownership and organised labour. The same process was also underway in Ireland, only here it was called Social Partnership.

The roots of the current housing crisis lie in this earlier period of public spending cuts and privatisation. During this period developers and banks consolidated themselves as the dominant wing of Irish capitalism which exerted huge influence on every level of government. It is no coincidence that so many of the scandals of this period related to the sell off and rezoning of publically owned land. For example, around 30% of zoned building land was owned by local authorities in the Dublin area in the 1970s. In 2006, just prior to the crash, the proportion had failed to just nine per cent. This was a not just a consequence of corrupt relationships between politicians – although those certainly did exist – but part of a conscious effort to convert land and houses into financial assets.

This process of financialisation continued on through the 1990's and reached a frenzy during the property boom of the early years of the current century. The governments of the period were instrumental in fuelling a speculative bubble through the introduction of property related tax breaks and the further deregulation of the banking sector. Spurred on by tax breaks, speculation and profiteering house prices increased from a ratio of four times the average industrial wage in 1996 to ten times it in 2007. Despite warning signs the government continued to maintain that the problem was lack of supply and that builders and developers must be incentivised to build more houses. As they rushed to get in on the pyramid scheme before it inevitably collapsed, the end result was ghost estates and 230,000 empty houses.

Despite this experience the very same arguments – of the need to incentivise capital investment in order to increase supply – are still being made today. However, the number of vacant properties testifies to the bogus nature of such claims. The housing crisis is not a question of supply and demand or of the market not operating correctly – for the class of people who own financial assets the market is working – the value of their assets is rising and profitability is increasing. The Irish government is doing all it can to ensure this is the case through tax breaks, the sale of NAMA assets and guarantees on rental incomes for landlords.

Rather than increase supply, an inflated housing market requires new house building to be severely restrained. In 2016 there was a new build output of approximately 14,800 compared with 14,602 in 2010. So in the period of the so called recovery new house building is only marginally higher than in the depths of the recession. Even as recently as 2009 when GDP was contracting significantly output was 26,402.

Another of feature of the new build figures is the very low rate of social housing building. Despite lengthening waiting lists – which now stand at 100,000 people across the state – new social housing is now almost non-existent. The total of local authority and housing association house-building construction in housing output has sharply contracted – going from 28% in 1985 to 6% in 2012. A total of just 75 were built in the year 2015. In Dublin city only 96 new homes have been finished over the past two years, despite the fact that the council owns enough land to accommodate 18,000 new units. The city centre has a waiting list of 22,203 people and accounts for 67 per cent of all homeless people in the country. At this rate of building it could take over 40 years to provide a permanent home to those on the Dublin City Council housing waiting list!

Between 2007 and 2015, real expenditure on public housing fell by nearly 63%, from a high of over €3.5 billion to approximately €1.3 billion. Gross capital formation by Government fell from almost €2.5 billion in 2007 to just over €600 million in 2015. However, the cuts to the social housing budget does not mean that there is no spending on housing. There certainly is but it has shifted to subsidies to owners of private property. So the collapse in spending on social housing has been paralleled by a surge in housing related benefits such as Rent Supplement and the Housing Assistance Payment as well as public subsidies to local authority tenants. This policy is based on rent supplements or subsidies to private landlords for renting to those in need of social housing. Such expenditure does not add to the stock of social housing but rather keeps a revenue flow to private landlords. The top 20 landlords now receive €5 million on an annual basis in rent allowance payments from the state. Last year, the overall amount paid out to hotels by Dublin City Council totalled €46.93m - a 20.5% jump on the €38.94m paid out in 2016. In addition, the council paid €12.3m to hostels and B&Bs. This is a very clear example of how the austerity programme works. It is not just about cuts – indeed in many cases the policies of austerity are more expensive- but about transferring resources from labour to capital, from one class of people to another.

The policies of the government in relation to housing cannot be understood without reference to the financial collapse and the Troika plan for the recovery of the Irish economy. This is based primarily on restoring the profitability of Irish banks and reducing their debt burden (of which developer loans and mortgages are central components). For this to work these financial assets must rise in value - house prices must increase, mortgage arrears must be recovered and properties must generate more revenues in the form of higher rents. This is key not only to aid the banks themselves but - related to this - in attracting international property investor and vulture funds to buy up formerly toxic loans and assets. The main mechanism in regard to this element of the recovery plan has been the sell off the residential and development land assets held by NAMA at knock-down prices.

Every government policy in relation to housing is designed to inflate the value of financial assets. Any polices that may mitigate against rising asset values such as rent controls, the expansion of public housing, or the transfer of NAMA properties to local councils must face this reality. Within the Troika framework there can be no solution to the housing crisis that is favourable to the working class. Indeed, the housing crisis is really just the continuation of the financial crash and bailout under which Irish workers are being made to pay for a crisis that was not of their making.

-IRELAND'S NEW LANDLORDISM

Absentee Landlords, Vulture Funds and NAMA.

Driving around the country, we are used to the sight of the crumbling remains of the mansions of many of the Anglo Irish landlord class. They are the result of an economic crisis and concerted waves of rebellion which resulted in these ferocious exploiters cutting their losses and selling off their land. Although the effects of that class and their particular brand of exploitation may appear to have faded in popular memory, scratch the surface and a consciousness of the evictions, imprisonments, transportation and emigration still exists.

Now emerging out of the banking bailout and the sale of distressed mortgages and property to vulture funds, a new 21st century landlord class is rapidly emerging which is every bit as voracious in its pursuit of profits as the 19th century landlords and every bit as callous.

The difference this time is that the landlords do not simply 'winter' in London or Bath. They are faceless, amorphous, global funds that can divest in a flash, leaving housing in Ireland at the whim of global interest rates and stock markets. They do not represent the tail end of an earlier form of land ownership in crisis due to evolving capitalist norms of agricultural production but are the parasitic expression of the ultimate, and most degraded, form of capitalism; Imperialism.

The arrival of the vulture funds on the Irish scene, carefully guided in by the new 'middlemen' of the Irish state, has sent a shiver through the Irish working masses. From small farming communities to the urban population that are paying exorbitant rents or struggling to pay mortgages the arrival of the new absentee landlord class casts over them a long and historically weighted shadow.

NAMA is being presented as an outstanding success, they have "disposed of most of the debt", are in line to make a profit for the State and Dublin's skyline is predicted to resemble that of London docklands or Singapore. The present expansion in construction is to a large extent the outworkings of the fire-sale of blocks of property to vulture funds by NAMA, and the distressed mortgages and debt is that which is being disposed of by banks that are seeking to deleverage quickly. The original owners have been compensated at anything up to 70% of their estimated value at the time and this has been paid by the Irish working people through pay cuts, pension cuts and taxes. The banks have walked away having taken a 'haircut', but having escaped taking full responsibility for their risk-taking and gambling.

The Irish State obligingly took over most of the banks speculative, loss making projects and has now sold them to vulture funds who, having collared a bargain, are set to benefit from rapidly expanding property prices. While as before the profits go to the speculators, financiers and landlords, the cost of this so called success is being borne overwhelmingly by working class people seeking a home and struggling to pay extortionate rents or to meet the costs of a mortgage.

The role of the State in preparing these conditions was starkly illustrated by the Department of Finance's activities, meeting with the vulture funds over 65 times in 2013 and 2014 while ignoring repeated requests for meetings with struggling mortgage holders and homeless groups. Indifferent to the pressing need for social housing following the crash, NAMA and the Department of Finance prioritised "attracting international capital".

The close relationship between the vulture funds and the Irish banking sector is indicated by the fact that Brian Goggins, previously a leading executive of the bailed out Bank of Ireland, later represented the Apollo fund property sell-off and played a key role in the talks between the fund and finance chief Michael Noonan.

Through Goggins and others the State openly encouraged these vulture funds to invest, setting up a Strategic Development Zone in the docklands area to attract them and leading NAMA's CEO to boast that:

> *"NAMA's market activity and deleveraging have contributed to the strong inflows of foreign capital".*

To assist this inflow, Real Estate Investment Trusts (REITs) were introduced in the 2013 budget in order to facilitate investment in 'high end' rental properties. The fear was that the supply of these properties would dry up and the inflow of vulture capital would end. REITs are limited on how much they can invest in development and it is here that the billions of Euro at NAMA's disposal was invested in partnership with the vulture funds at places like Docklands and Cherrywood.

With these mechanisms established and with NAMA's commitment to invest in major developments in order to keep the supply of suitable luxury properties flowing the vultures proceeded to circle and with a promised return of 15% – 20% per year, and virtually non existent taxation, the feeding frenzy was under way.

The Irish State was at the centre of these preparations, feting global investment funds while struggling working class people were left out in the cold. Money that could have provided social housing for working people on land already owned by the State instead primed the pump for global profiteers. Such is the nature of the 'recovery'.

This new absentee landlord class includes the Vulture fund Cerberus, which bought the 'Project Eagle' loans. Lone Star Capital, which now own Lloyds bad debts, Hines, a Texas based company, and King Street Capital of New York both of whom along with NAMA now owns the 400 acre Cherrywood development in South Dublin. I.RES, one of the largest real-estate investment trusts registered on the Irish stock exchange, backed by Canadian finance, now owns up to 3000 apartments snapped up from NAMA in 'Project Orange'. Oxley Holdings, Singapore, now own 72 – 80 North wall quay, and is planning on developing luxury apartments, while just across the river Liffey Kennedy Wilson, Los Angeles based, now part owns the Capital Docks project on Sir John Rogerson's Quay. All these firms are benefiting from NAMA's investment in the development of commercial or luxury accommodation. They also own the Clancy Quay complex and have numerous apartment blocks in the city. Other companies include Fir Tree Partners, and Marathon Asset Management. A number of different funds owned Clerys department store for a period before selling it off for development and sacking the 400 workers. These funds ultimately have snatched up 90% of what NAMA had for sale making them at present the largest landlords in the Irish state and they are continuing to grow as they snap up the banks remaining "nonperforming loans".

As the Banks' sale of nonperforming loans has gained momentum farm debt has also been drawn into the selloff. Around 200 farms have been placed in jeopardy by Ulster Bank's sale to Cerberus of its loan portfolio worth €2.5 billion in late 2016 with hundreds more expecting the same fate.

It is housing that is worst effected however. People generally had no other option than buy at the height of the boom and at hugely inflated prices. Many of these same people, who are now still suffering the effects of the collapse and subsequent austerity, find themselves struggling to pay large mortgages which show up on the books as nonperforming loans despite various mechanisms and agreements with the banks that allow for flexibility in repayments. It is these "distressed" debts that are being presented to the vultures as the source of a quick profit.

Fire-sales of distressed debt have proceeded at an accelerating pace since the sale of Tyrrellstown, which effected 40 tenants, to the latest tranche which sees 14,000 mortgages being made available for sale by the 75% State owned PTSB. The vulture funds are not regulated by the Central Bank so it is unclear exactly how many mortgages they hold at present but it has been estimated that we may see up to 30,000 home repossessions in the coming period as mortgage holders in arrears are pushed into insolvency and are evicted.

With Irish banks still carrying over 25% of nonperforming loans on their books they are coming under increasing pressure from the ECB to offload them in order to pass 'stress tests', improve their ability to withstand another shock and to increase their issuance of new "performing" debt. It is estimated that up to 100,000 mortgages are in arrears and their sale to vulture funds is the banks preferred method to return their balance sheets to health.

The vultures are thriving. House price inflation has pushed newbuild three bedroom houses in Dublin to over €800,000 while the most modest accommodation costs anything between €250,000 to €750,000 depending on location. This has forced people who cannot get such a large mortgage on to the top end of the burgeoning rental sector and allowed the new landlords to push rents ever higher. The result has been that many struggling renters have been forced to return to their parental homes and sometimes into emergency accommodation and those that are barely hanging on to mortgages are facing eviction to facilitate resales.

The vulture funds would not invest in housing in a society where everyone is guaranteed a secure comfortable home. A shortage of housing and skyrocketing rents suits them, so the Irish State by refusing to address the need for adequate public housing guarantees their market.

It is precisely this acute housing shortage that makes the investment in Dublin apartment blocks all the more attractive to the vultures. The Department of Finance's efforts has encouraged them to invest in a distressed housing market that is also being carefully managed by the State to protect their interests while divesting the banks of nonperforming loans at the expense of the very real human distress of homeless or struggling families.

These global investors are in search of short term profits with a typical term of around five to seven years and in the case of Irish housing they have a target of 15 – 20% return on their investments irrespective of the social consequences. Such generous returns are achieved in part by repossessions and resale, or evictions and re-lets at ever increasing rents and they are turning fabulous profits. Just one of the smaller investment vehicles, the Green REIT, has reported a profit of €53 million for the 6 months to December 2017, 21% up on the same period in 2016.

Calls for quotas of affordable housing to be built by developers or even the State is not enough. 'Affordable' is a vague term when it is dependent upon the vagaries of the capitalist market and the greed driven developers that got us into this mess in the first place. The capitalist State's first responsibility is to the protection of capital and that means sticking to its plans to reduce State spending to less than 60% of GDP or, as has been mooted by Michael Noonan before his departure, a reduction to a revised figure of 45% of GDP.

But the priorities and needs of the working class are fundamentally counterposed to these objectives. During the famine tonnes of foodstuffs were shipped out of the country to keep the landlords' profits up while people were evicted, emigrated and starved. Although not of the same magnitude of severity the relationship between the new landlord class and the working people that stand in the way of their profits today also remains one of callous indifference.

The thousands of acres and millions of Euro owned by the taxpayers through NAMA could be used to build houses with controlled rents in places central to Dublin where people need to live in order to work. But not only would building thousands of social homes push the State to break out of the limits of the Troika's fiscal space, it could also harm demand and therefore harm the interests of the preferred method of recovery, the vulture funds, which the State systematically set out to attract. The need for adequate social housing clashes with the need for profit.

The "recovery" is entirely dependent upon the immiseration of the working class. It is firmly based on the age old maxim that 'the rich get richer and the poor get poorer' and as part of that recovery the banks seek to offload their non performing mortgages to vulture funds at a discount. The banks benefit by having healthier balance sheets allowing them to expand their mortgage lending again, the vultures benefit by a quick turnaround of its purchases or huge hikes in rental income in an inflating market where there is a housing shortage. Working class people needing a house or struggling to maintain a mortgage are once again to be bled white to provide the banks and corporations with profits, no matter what the human cost!

Talk of regulating these parasitic global giants is just so much hot air, especially coming from Fianna Fail and the like who seek to apply a little window dressing to Irish capitalism's strategy for "recovery" and to rehabilitate themselves.

What is needed is not some half-hearted regulation at a snail's pace or quotas of jerrybuilt "affordable" housing for those in a position to bury themselves in debt again to the banks, but quality social housing for all who need it.

"Off balance sheet alternatives" and "good vulture funds" are just another form of bank bailout when what is needed is mortgage debt forgiveness for the struggling working people who have already subsidised the banks through their pay and pension cuts and their taxes.

The vulture funds that are now benefiting from State intervention in major building projects in Ireland have invested heavily in distressed debt throughout Europe, aggravating a housing shortage that sees 78% of young Danes and 65% of young Germans spending over 40% of their income on housing while overall 10% of Europeans spend 50% of their income on keeping a roof over their heads. Globally, the vultures are draining profits from Africa and South America, including Argentina and Puerto Rico, through economic collapse and natural disaster respectively, anywhere there is real human distress.

This is how capitalism is "recovering" and it is this global imperialist capital which the Irish State has carefully opened the door for, paving its way towards the struggling mortgage holders and bad debt that is the legacy of the property bubble and the crash. The system that caused the catastrophe, its bankers, property developers and speculators have been refinanced and supported but their victims, the people who had no option but to buy at hugely inflated prices, are now to go the way of Clerys workforce. Thrown out!

Eviction in Ireland has always been confronted by communities and doggedly resisted. The occupation of NAMA land and property as before at the 2016 Apollo House occupation has clearly pointed the way towards an effective fight back. As in the water charge protests local people physically stopped the meters going in, the same tactic can stop tenants being moved out. Community mobilisation against evictions is the most practical tool of all and this is already beginning to happen in local communities.

Resistance to eviction is an aspect of class struggle which traditionally has risen to prominence during periods of acute industrial action when landlords used evictions to defend not only their own profits but capitalist profits in general by attempting to crush striking workers morale. It is a class issue, an important part of the confrontation between capital and the working class and trade unionists, especially bank workers, must refuse to participate in the process of eviction in any way. The operation of the Permanent TSB fund would be seriously hit if the trade unions withdrew their labour in protest at the sale of mortgages to the vultures, but the leadership of the trade unions are refusing to budge.

The trade union leadership's refusal to act is due to their political perspective. They favour "off balance sheet" solutions because they have signed up to capitalism's recovery plan by keeping trade union demands commensurate with the agreed "fiscal space". This 'space' prohibits adequate social housing provision, so in order to avoid having to break out of their tacit agreement with capitalist strategy they have established an arms-length relationship with housing campaigns. Fighting the vulture funds means breaking out of that fiscal space and building houses in the numbers that will end the housing crisis and leave the vultures nothing to feed on. But where is the profit in that?

A housing campaign for social housing for all who need it must confront the trade union bureaucracy and the reformist lefts' tacit acceptance of these fiscal parameters laid down by the capitalist recovery plan.

Solidarity can win if it makes the vultures' investments too expensive for them to maintain and their demands for evictions impossible to implement. The alternative of waiting for the State to half-heartedly "regulate" the very vampires they have been inviting in since 2013 will, as they very well know, leave any amelioration of the debt sell offs too late for most of its victims.

In the meantime, no one must be evicted, people need houses so they must be built and the large stock of unused and speculative property should be occupied.

THE HOUSING CRISIS IN THE NORTH OF IRELAND

In relation to the overall Irish housing crisis the Northern enclave is seen as something of a sideshow. Given its status as a colony, the Northern housing crisis is refracted through the British economy. It was therefore something of a surprise to find that a block of NAMA property with a book price of over 4 billion was held in the North.

It was less surprising to learn that, mirroring developments in the South, the property block had been sold to the Cerberus vulture fund for one quarter of its book price amid allegations of corruption, payments to a NAMA official and millions deposited in an offshore account linked to a major figure in the Democratic Unionist party.

The promise of the Good Friday agreement and the St. Andrews agreement that followed it, the political foundations of the settlement in the North, was that the end of the troubles would bring a peace dividend and economic boom. In reality the sectarian settlement, rather than overseeing the profits of peace, was dominated by the sharing of the spoils of war between Sinn Fein and the Democratic Unionist party. This was replicated throughout society leading to widespread corruption. Rather than economic growth we saw a speculative property boom followed by a property bust.

Ironically the republican struggle kept Thatcherism at bay. It was argued that massive public sector cuts such as those in Britain would simply fuel mass resentment and further support for the Republicans. Today austerity rolls forward unchecked. A gain of the earlier civil rights struggle had been the formation of the Housing Executive. The Unionist Councils had failed to build housing and, because the house was linked to the local government vote they provided housing for Catholics only with the greatest reluctance. Following the establishment of the executive, the provision of large-scale public sector housing was of immense benefit to all workers, but the new body collaborated with the police and other state forces in enforcing widespread housing apartheid. Today the role of the executive has been scaled back in a move towards privatisation. New housing is shifting to Housing associations who finance themselves on the open market and lead the move towards market rules. At the same time the involvement of "community" groups in the new bodies opens them to further sectarian division. In the meantime the Housing executive and the other state organs continue to support housing apartheid, to ignore the activity of loyalist gangsters and to oversee constant threats and evictions of migrants and of Catholics who settle in the "wrong" area.

The Northern homeless situation is on a par with the South. The published figures for 2016 showed that some 18,600 households were officially recognised as Homeless, some 11,200 were recognised by the Housing Executive as 'Full Duty Applicants,' i.e. genuinely high priority, eligible for assistance and unintentionally homeless. In Belfast five people died sleeping on the streets in 2015. It is estimated that there are at least 80,000 living as 'concealed adults'; this means people living in the homes of others on a temporary basis. Meanwhile the number of prospective Social Housing units available has fallen steadily across the North, the Housing Executive now builds about 2,000 new units per annum because of financial and statutory restraints. The lack of affordable social housing has engendered a panic in the private rented sector and this sector has quadrupled in size in just ten years. It is often said that the North has a high density of social housing. This is not true. the correct figure is 16% for the North, 17% for England and 24% for Scotland. The Northern Ireland Executive staggered the introduction of the more stringent welfare cuts, including the bedroom tax until 2020. When these do finally take hold in tandem with the introduction of the Universal Credit benefit reform, homelessness and general housing distress will certainly get much worse.

The political settlement has been changed over the years to increase housing distress through the added factor of sectarian horsetrading when it comes to house building and allocation. The nationalist community currently constitute 45 percent of the Belfast City area, yet they constitute 75 percent of those existing in objective one housing need. Under the Good Friday Agreement all Government departments were in theory required to actively redress religious inequality by considering such objective evidence, but that is not what was done.

The hard evidence certainly exists that the rules on 'fairness' were not honoured. North Belfast contains six out of the 20 most deprived income wards in the North of Ireland. As of 2005 there were 789 Catholics considered by the Housing Executive to be in objective need, the figure for Protestants being 179. That figure climbed to 1081 and 403 respectively by 2011. However in 2011 the Northern Ireland Housing Executive under pressure from the DUP was obliged to waive its policy of building new social homes on the basis of objective need criteria, instead allocation for North Belfast was to be based a strictly 50/50 religious basis. This new criteria was used to block the required allocation of potential new homes to Catholics on the site of the old Girdwood army barracks and Crumlin Road Gaol. In 2011 a plan was initiated to build a large community centre on the Girdwood site with many fewer houses, with provision for just 60 new homes. What was especially interesting about this sectarian stitch up was how put in place with the help of Sinn Fein, the MLA for the area Gerry Kelly was quoted in the local radio as saying:

> 'We are deliberately not talking about the numbers involved.'

Alongside sectarian deals went collusion with business in maintaining "land banks". The issue of leaving spare land free when so many are in dire need was raised at a meeting of Belfast City Council on 15th August 2017 when once again planning permission was given to another 'brown field' site for retail use only. This was despite the fact that there had been a heavy presence of campaigners including single mothers in desperate need of housing who had waited three hours to plea for more homes before the application was heard.

Finally in 2015, powers to make decisions on housing and planning were handed back to the local Councils after more than 40 years since those powers were taken away for good reason. As the councils are not constrained by the limited vetoes that apply in the fallen executive, this can only be described as a totally backward step to an even more sectarian time, this decision was also approved of by Sinn Fein.

Today the political settlement in the north of Ireland is in a state of collapse and will not be revived short of an absolute Sinn Fein capitulation to unionism. Economically the landscape is dominated by the fresh start agreement, which brings in, in one tranche, all the misery visited on British workers over years to an area that stands at the bottom of the economic league table.

As in the South, trade union leaders accept the fresh start austerity. However in the South ICTU argues that they have ameliorated the worst of austerity through collaboration. In the North the only form of amelioration is a hardship fund that delays full implementation of the cuts. The union leaderships are reduced to arguing that the workers should sacrifice themselves in order to save the local executive. They hold to this even though the executive has collapsed, arguing now that the sectarian carve up should be restored so that it can serve the needs of the workers! In a similar way Sinn Fein, standing as the left voice against austerity in the South, claim the northern austerity is caused by British cuts while they continue to support them.

In the North to an even greater extent than in the South we see the political and economic collapse of a system alongside the lack of any political alternative. This situation is not sustainable and it is likely that the shock of Brexit will bring the whole house of cards tumbling to the ground.

A RADICAL MOVEMENT, A RADICAL STRATEGY:

Lessons of Apollo House

Many assume that the model of the right2water campaign, claimed by the National Homeless and Housing Coalition, provides a template for the battle around housing. The claims of the group are open to question. The main force behind the coalition, The Services Industrial Professional and Technical Union (SIPTU) was a minor force in right2water, mainly because its leader, Jack O'Connor, always supported a process of behind the scenes lobbying of government and as a result of previous deals continued to support water charging. SIPTU now argue that a broad movement could maximize support and apply the greatest pressure on the government. That view has led to controversy, with activists arguing that SIPTU's support for a Labour party presence in the campaign compromises the new campaign, as Labour in government helped cause the housing crisis.

The role of SIPTU shows that, while the union leaders may be the last line of defence for the workers, they are also far too willing to sign off on deals that leave workers at a disadvantage. Recent actions by teachers in the US and university lecturers in Britain show that toleration for the quiet deal is evaporating and that when it does workers can successfully push back.

With hindsight there were many weaknesses in the right2water movement. Its aims were unclear and no real democratic structures were built. The union leadership looked to a new deal with government, with all the risks associated with laying down your weapons before the battle was won.

So water charging was postponed for the majority, but Irish Water survived, as did the charging structure and the roadmap to privatisation.

Can we do better with housing? Above all we need clear radical aims that will meet the needs of Irish workers.

From that point of view the housing and homelessness campaign call for a housing emergency is too broad. It ignores the continuing observance of Troika rules that hold public spending in narrow confines, ignores the banker's debt we will pay for decades, avoids criticism of the utter reliance of the government on market mechanisms and is blind to the open collaboration between government and Vulture capital that is a major driver of homelessness.

We support the Campaign for Public Housing in its call for a mass programme of social housing. Given the governments support for landlordism and its role as an agent of the Troika, we need to go beyond lobbying the authorities to a policy of civil disobedience and direct action. The way to decide a strategy is to unite all the different groups of activists in a single campaign that presents a radical programme meeting the needs of the workers rather than those of the financiers and build a democratic campaign where we can discuss differences and unite around a common strategy.

Who is the target of government policy? Who is it who is threatened by the Irish Housing Crisis? It is not just the army of rough sleepers on our streets and the shocking level of sudden death in the winter months. Nor is it simply an issue of the "hidden homeless" moving from couch to couch in a desperate struggle to avoid rough sleeping. It doesn't stop with the young parents, trapped in Bed and Breakfast rooms, struggling to meet their children's needs in impossible conditions.

The housing crisis affects the mass of working people, living in fear of eviction, of the next rent increase or the next rise in mortgage interest rate. Wondering when they will no longer have the reserves to put food on the table. This is the central issue. Out of control rents, high mortgages, Vulture capitalism and the Troika rules are all working together to produce a downward pressure on real wages. Without a fight there will be another decade of austerity and penury for the majority of workers.

So what's the solution? Do we call on the government to speed up the market? Offer more incentives? More regulation? Rent control? Demand more social housing? We should certainly call for reform, but we must bear in mind the role of the government in the protection of landlordism, its role in the mass sell-off of NAMA properties and its alliance with the European bankers and the vulture capitalists. It will take enormous effort to wring anything from them.

What's wrong with the Apollo House strategy? At the end of 2016 a coalition of trade unionists and housing activists seized the empty Apollo House office complex; NAMA property, OUR property, paid for by the Irish working class, and used it to house the homeless.

It was wildly popular, but ended after concessions that ran alongside threats from the courts

It's time for round two and this has opened with a coalition of housing activists and students seizing a property at Summerhill Parade in Dublin, the subject of mass eviction and now held empty as a speculative investment There will be confrontation with courts, bailiffs and guards, but we know enough history to know that this conflict is inevitable and enough combatively to know that with enough support we can win.

However further steps are needed. We have to face up to the fact that Ireland is a country dominated by imperialism where local rulers act as agents to further the exploitation of Irish workers. To deal with this reality we need a party of the working class that, in the struggle between profit and worker's needs, always unhesitatingly stands with the workers.

A working class government would in all cases put people before property rights. A working class party, a united movement, would apply the Apollo House strategy of repudiating the outstanding debts arising from the banking guarantee and going forward to seize public property, paid for by the workers, to meet housing needs.

Printed in Great Britain
by Amazon